CW00362002

feasts

by Joe Inglis

Public Eye Publications

A Public Eye Publications Book

www.thegreatestintheworld.com

Design and layout: The DesignCouch
www.designcouch.co.uk

Editor: Steve Brookes

Copy editor: Bronwyn Robertson
www.theartsva.com

This first edition published in 2007 by
Public Eye Publications, PO Box 3182,
Stratford-upon-Avon, Warwickshire CV37 7XW

A CIP catalogue record for this book is available from the British Library
ISBN 9781-905151-14-1

Printed and bound by Biddles Books Limited, King's Lynn, Norfolk PE30 4LS

dedicated to Jill

The most mischevious but adorable tabby cat in the world!

introduction

Cats have two great loves in life – sleeping and eating. Sleeping they can take care of themselves very nicely, but when it comes to eating, our pet cats are totally in our hands. In the wild, cats live on a diet of small rodents, which gives them just the right mix of fresh protein, minerals and vitamins they need. But we're not so keen on providing our cats with a ready supply of mice, so we feed them on convenient complete foods.

Many of these complete diets are made up of some pretty unhealthy ingredients however, including chemicals, additives and preservatives, as well as using low-grade protein sources such as 'meat and animal derivatives' instead of the real meat cats thrive on. Cats can survive on these foods – but they are far from ideal for their long-term health and happiness.

As a vet, I believe that high quality natural foods are the best and healthiest way to feed our pets. Avoiding chemical additives and using real meat as the main source of protein are the cornerstones of a healthy diet for a cat – which is why I've created this recipe book, and also developed my own natural complete food for cats, 'Joe & Jill's'.

I've created the recipes in this book using my veterinary knowledge – and the helping whiskers of my cat Jill, who's had a paw in every dish! They're not designed to be replacements for your cat's complete diet – more occasional treats designed to light up her week and add a little healthy variety to her life.

Just remember though, that cats are the fussiest creatures in the world, so whilst all these recipes have been puss-approved by Jill, not all of them will be to your cat's taste. The only way to find out what tickles her taste buds is to try out a few and see what happens – and once you find those that she loves, you'll have one contented and healthy cat on your hands!

Enjoy!

Joe Inglis

contents

Before you start…

Cooking for your cat is not exactly rocket science, but there are a few things it's important to be aware of, especially if you're thinking about experimenting with some of your own recipes.

Firstly, cats have a very specific biological requirement for meat, and they can't survive without several key amino-acids (the building blocks of protein) which are only found in meat. So a vegetarian diet for a cat is not a realistic option – stick to recipes which are meat based.

Secondly, when you're cooking for cats, you have to try to put yourself in your cat's mind when it comes to flavours and textures. Remember that a cat's idea of what's tasty is very different from ours, and so many of the recipes in this book might not sound very attractive to you (liver and banana milkshake anyone…?) but they'll go down a treat with your cat. So when you're coming up with your own recipes, think cat and come up with dishes which are rich in meaty and fishy smells.

Thirdly, there are some slightly unusual ingredients in some of these recipes, which need a quick introduction:

 Catnip – this herb is a relative of garden mint, and is available from good health stores. It contains a chemical called nepetalactone which drives most cats into a brief frenzy of excited activity. Not all cats are affected, so if your cat turns up his nose at a catnip recipe, don't be offended – it's just in his genes.

 Brewer's yeast – this is the pasteurised residue of commercial brewed beer and packed full of all sorts of nutrients. Buy it in powder or tablet form from your local health store.

 Marmite (or other yeast extracts) – like brewer's yeast, these extracts are very rich in protein and vitamins. They also have the added bonus of being very strong tasting and most cats love the meaty flavour.

And finally, a quick word on ingredients that are best avoided. Some of the foods listed below will just cause the odd upset stomach – but some, like onion and mushroom, can be fatal in exceptional circumstances – so it's vital you check out any recipe to make sure it's safe.

 Tomatoes – a small amount of ripe tomato is unlikely to cause any problems, but green tomatoes can cause serious stomach upsets and even heart problems, so it's best to avoid them.

 Onions (and garlic to a lesser degree) – can cause blood problems including anaemia. Again small amounts are very unlikely to cause any problems, but to be on the safe side I only use small amounts of garlic and very little onion in my recipes.

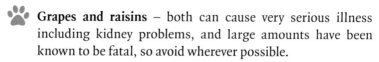 **Grapes and raisins** – both can cause very serious illness including kidney problems, and large amounts have been known to be fatal, so avoid wherever possible.

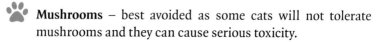 **Mushrooms** – best avoided as some cats will not tolerate mushrooms and they can cause serious toxicity.

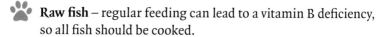 **Raw fish** – regular feeding can lead to a vitamin B deficiency, so all fish should be cooked.

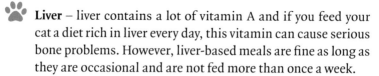 **Liver** – liver contains a lot of vitamin A and if you feed your cat a diet rich in liver every day, this vitamin can cause serious bone problems. However, liver-based meals are fine as long as they are occasional and are not fed more than once a week.

everyday meals

Treating your cat to a healthy home cooked meal once a week is a great way of rewarding her for all that affection and love she gives to you. While good quality natural complete food should make up the majority of your cat's diet, as it contains the ideal mix of nutrients to keep her healthy, there's nothing better than a good dose of fresh food every now and then to keep her in the very best shape.

Cook up one of these delicious meals for your cat and she'll be the happiest (and healthiest) cat in town!

meaty rice delight

Jill absolutely loves this recipe – and it's not just tasty, it's really healthy as well as it contains pretty much all the essential nutrients cats depend on. Make up a big batch and then store it in the freezer in single-serving bags. Because it contains liver, I'd recommend feeding it once a week at most.

YOU'LL NEED (to make enough for approx 10 servings)

- 100g rice
- 2 teaspoons corn oil
- 250g beef, minced
- 1 egg
- 100g liver, diced

1 Boil the rice according to the instructions on the packet, drain and leave to cool. Meanwhile fry the mince and liver in the oil for about five minutes, until brown and cooked through. Then break in the egg (but don't discard the shell) and stir vigorously over a moderate heat for another couple of minutes, before setting mixture to one side to cool.

2 While the meat is cooling, put the egg shell on a baking tray and cook in a hot oven for five minutes. This will kill off any nasty bugs such as salmonella and also make it easier to grind up, which is the next step.

3 Using either a pestle and mortar or rolling pin, crush up the shell until it forms a powder, and sprinkle 1 level teaspoon into the rice. This provides calcium for healthy bones, as meat and rice are both quite low in this essential mineral.

4 Finally, mix the meat and egg into the rice and blend together thoroughly. Serve in small portions with a little of your cat's normal dried food as a side dish to add a bit of crunch to the meal.

NUTRITION TIP

Grapes and raisins might look harmless enough but they can be fatal to cats so avoid them in all recipes destined for your cat's dish!

chewy chicken biscuits

There's nothing that our cat likes more than to start her day with a handful of these crunchy biscuits. In fact Jill likes them so much, she once managed to open the kitchen cupboard and get the lid off the plastic box they were in. I found her in the morning sitting guiltily on the kitchen floor, surrounded by crumbs!

Luckily, as these biscuits are really healthy, Jill was absolutely fine. You can feed these everyday like I do, but make sure that your cat still gets plenty of her normal food as these biscuits aren't a replacement for a complete diet.

YOU'LL NEED

- 60g rice
- 60g wholemeal flour
- 2 tablespoons vegetable oil
- ½ chicken stock cube
- 225g chicken mince
- ½ teaspoon brewer's yeast
- ½ teaspoon dried kelp
- A little cooking oil

1. Cook the rice, drain and allow to cool. Then mix it together with the flour, oil and crumbled stock cube. Brown the mince gently in a frying pan and then add in to the mix, along with the brewer's yeast and kelp. Then add hot water a little at a time, until the mixture is wet enough to form a thick and heavy dough.

2. Wet your hands and then roll up the mixture into grape-sized balls which you drop onto a well-greased baking tray. Bake in a moderate oven (180°C/350°F/Gas 4) for about 25 minutes, until the biscuits are firm and golden brown. Allow to cool well before brushing with a little oil (to add a bit of extra palatability) and serving as a morning treat.

3. These biscuits keep well in an airtight container for at least a week.

 fish fingers

Who out there doesn't have a soft spot for good old fish fingers? Most people, I would have thought, and it probably won't surprise you to learn that our feline friends are pretty partial to the occasional fish finger too.

This recipe is great because it uses oily fish like mackerel or pilchards which are full of omega-3 fatty acids. These 'good fats' benefit the whole body, from brain to tail, so a weekly serving of this recipe will keep your cat in tiptop condition.

YOU'LL NEED (to make ten cat-sized fish fingers)

- 1 tin of fish such as mackerel or pilchards (approx 120g)
- 50g wholegrain breadcrumbs
- 1 tablespoon oil
- 1 egg
- 1 tablespoon plain flour
- 1 teaspoon brewer's yeast (optional)

1 All you need to do is to mix everything together in a large bowl until it forms a sticky dough (wet your hands for this, otherwise it will stick to you like glue!) Then form it into about ten finger shapes on a well-greased baking tray and bake in a moderate oven for 20 minutes, turning once.

2 Once cool, serve with a little portion of fishy cat food for a fantastic feline feast!

3 Keep leftover fingers in the fridge for up to five days – not that any self-respecting cat will allow you to leave them that long without pestering you to bits!

Did you know ...
that tinned cat foods are about 80% water? That might sound a lot, but it's about the same as fresh meat!

chicken & tuna stew

This is a great winter recipe for those cats who love to spend the day out mousing or exploring, before coming in to wolf down a hearty meal and then lie in front of the fire. Serve up a helping of this stew on its own, or on top of his normal dried food, and you will have one contented cat on you hands (or, more likely, on your sofa!).

YOU'LL NEED (enough to serve several cats)

- 1 chicken drumstick
- 1 small carrot, grated
- ½ teaspoon mixed herbs
- ½ small tin tuna

1. Brown the chicken drumstick in a medium sized saucepan, using a little oil. Add in the grated carrot and continue to fry for a few minutes. Then pour over just enough water to cover and bring to the boil. Add in the herbs at this point. Reduce the heat and simmer for 45 minutes (adding more water as required to keep the chicken covered).

2. Then allow to cool before removing the chicken and deboning it. Sieve out the carrot from the broth and mix it with the meat and tuna in a large bowl. Then pour in 1 cup of the broth and mix again to form a thick and chunky soup. Garnish with a little catnip if you have some, and serve warm.

Catnip can drive some cats wild. It contains a chemical called nepetalactone which drives most cats into a brief frenzy of excited activity. Not all cats are affected though, so if your cat turns his nose up at a catnip recipe, don't be offended – it's just in his genes.

mini fish balls with fishy gravy

Obviously not one for the cat who doesn't like fish, but for most cats this is their idea of food heaven. The combination of the fleshy fish balls with the strong-tasting gravy is enough to drive even the pickiest cat wild – and not only that, it's good for them as well!

YOU'LL NEED (to make enough for 3–4 cats)

- 2 whole sardines or 1 small mackerel
- 1 teaspoon oil
- ½ carrot, grated
- 1 tablespoon cornflour
- Salty water

1 First you need to fillet the fish. The easiest way to do this is to remove the skin, head and tail with a knife, and then break away the flesh using a teaspoon. Once most of the flesh is off, put the skin, head and tail into a saucepan with the oil and brown gently for 2 minutes. Add the grated carrot and continue to fry for a couple of minutes. Then add in 1 pint of water and bring to the boil. Simmer gently for about half an hour.

2 While the stock is cooking, take the fish and set about it with a rolling pin or the flat surface of a large kitchen knife. The idea is to pulverise it as much as possible – just be careful not to pulverise your fingers (or the cat's paw if he's trying to help!). Then add in the cornflour and about 4 tablespoons of warm water – just enough to make a thick and sticky paste. Form the paste into small balls and dip each in some salty water.

3 Once the stock has had its thirty minutes of simmering, fish out all the bones and head (but leave in any soft bits like fins, skin or very well cooked and soft bones). Then drop in the fish balls and let them cook for about five minutes before turning off the heat and letting it cool for at least an hour. Then, when you're fed up with the cats pestering you, give in and serve a small portion with two or three balls and a tablespoon of gravy to each cat.

 liver & rice pâté

The liver is the engine of the body, carrying out hundreds of vital tasks, so it's not surprising that it's full of healthy nutrients. It's especially rich in vitamins (including vitamins A, B, D, E and K) and minerals, as well as providing a good source of protein and fatty acids.

This pâté recipe combines all the goodness of liver with the easily digestible energy from rice, to make a tasty treat that's ideal as an occasional meal.

YOU'LL NEED

- 60g rice
- 100g liver (lamb or chicken)
- 1 teaspoon dried kelp
- A little milk or cream

1   The best way to cook the rice and liver is to boil them together in a pan of water. This allows all the flavour of the liver to soak into the rice, giving the whole pâté extra taste. Chop the liver into chunks and then boil with the rice until the rice is tender.

2 Drain away the water and pour the rice and liver into a blender, along with the kelp (this is dried seaweed which is an excellent source of iodine, essential for your cat's thyroid gland – don't add this though if your cat has an over-active thyroid, a condition called *hyperthyroidism*).

3 Blend everything together until it forms a rich pâté, adding a little milk or cream as required. Form it into a nice shaped mould if you're feeling artistic – or just spoon onto a plate if you're not! Pop it in the fridge to cool and serve with a sprinkling of dried kibble on top.

Did you know ...

that the fattest cat on record is Himmy, a tabby from Redlynch, Queensland, Australia. Himmy weighed over 20kg, and died in 1986 at 10 years of age!

cheesy chicken pasta bake

Most cats love cheese and the addition of a teaspoon of Marmite into this recipe makes this a winner with every cat I've tried it on (with the possible exception of Lilly the Birman who did turn her nose up at it – but she only eats fresh fish from her owner's hand, so it wasn't really a fair test!).

You can freeze this, so make up a dish full and bag it up into single servings and store until next time.

YOU'LL NEED

- **150g pasta** (any shape will do)
- **150g chicken mince**
- **60g cheddar cheese, grated**
- **300ml milk**
- **20g plain flour**
- **20g butter**
- **¼ teaspoon Marmite**

---

1 Cook the pasta according to the instructions on the packet and once drained, set it aside to cool.

2 Meanwhile, make a start on the cheesy chicken sauce by melting the butter in a small pan over a low heat. Stir in the flour and gently cook for 2–3 minutes.

3 Remove the sauce from the heat and gradually add in the milk, stirring continuously to avoid lumps. Return to the heat and bring to the boil, still stirring, and simmer for five minutes, stirring occasionally. When smooth and creamy, stir in the cheese a little at a time until melted.

4 Brown the chicken mince in a frying pan (you shouldn't need any oil as there is plenty of fat in the mince), and, after five minutes or so, add it into the cheese sauce along with the Marmite. Mix it all in together and then pour over the pasta in an ovenproof dish. Bake in a moderate oven for about 25 minutes, until brown on top, and then set aside to cool thoroughly before serving.

NUTRITION TIP

Always make sure your cat has a good clean source of fresh water available – after oxygen, water is the second most vital requirement for all animals, cats included.

everyday meals

homemade turkey kibbles

There's nothing better for your cat's teeth than crunching on hard foods such as dried kibbles. But feeding the same old biscuits day after day can get a little dull for the cat, so here's a recipe for some healthy home-cooked kibbles that can be mixed in with his normal dinner, or fed as an alternative every now and then.

YOU'LL NEED

- **250g turkey mince**
- **100g rice** (brown is healthier than white)
- **1 small carrot, grated**
- **1 dessertspoon oil**
- **1 egg**
- **½ teaspoon brewer's yeast** (optional)

1 Boil the rice according to the instructions on the packet, and when it's cooked, drain off the water and leave it to stand.

2 Meanwhile, fry up the carrot in the oil for a few minutes before adding the mince and cooking over a gentle heat for 7–10 minutes.

3 Beat the egg into the rice, but don't throw away the shell. Instead, drop it into a small pan of boiling water and let it simmer for five minutes, just to make sure it's sterile.

4. Drain the water and then grind up the shell up in a pestle and mortar or under a rolling pin until it forms a fine powder. Add about ½ a teaspoon of the powder to the rice mixture. This adds calcium to the kibbles, balancing the relatively low-calcium mince and rice.

5. Next, mix the cooked carrot, mince (and brewer's yeast if you have some) into the rice mixture in a blender and give it a whiz until it forms a thick paste. Set aside to cool. Meanwhile put the oven on to warm up (200°C/400°F/Gas 6).

6. Then grease a baking tray or two, and form the mixture into small kibbles. You can either do this using wet hands, which works well but takes quite a long time, or by squeezing the mixture through the holes in a potato masher, which is quicker. Place the kibbles on the baking trays and put them in the oven for 60 minutes, until they are hard and crunchy.

Adjust your cat's daily food intake according to their lifestyle – active cats who spend their lives outdoors may need up to 50% more food than a lazy lap cat who snoozes by the fire all day!

 chicken kiev

This quick and easy recipe is based on a traditional Chicken Kiev, but I've changed the garlic filling to a more cat-friendly fish paste and catnip mixture. It's very healthy, with lean chicken meat and fish protein from the paste – and as long as your cat is one of those that adores catnip, it's a sure-fire winner in the taste department too!

YOU'LL NEED (for one large kitty meal)

- 1 small chicken breast
- 1 jar fish paste
- ¼ teaspoon catnip
- 1 tablespoon plain flour
- 1 egg, beaten
- Breadcrumbs

1 Slit open the chicken breast along its length and fold it open. Place a teaspoon of fish paste in the middle, sprinkle in most of the catnip and close the chicken back together to form a neat parcel.

2 Cover the chicken with the flour, dip it in the beaten egg, and roll it in the breadcrumbs to finish the Kiev. Then place it on a greased baking tray and cook for half an hour at (180°C/350°F/Gas 4). Serve, once cooled, with a garnish of catnip

everyday meals

 stewed lamb

Cats don't often eat lamb – it's not in many commercial cat foods – but that doesn't mean it's not good for them, or that they don't like it. In fact the opposite is true – most cats that I've ever owned, Jill included, have been great lamb fans, and as a meat it's pretty healthy, especially when compared with beef.

This stew combines lamb with liver for an extra shot of vitamins and minerals, and is another easy-to-freeze dish that can be whipped out whenever the cat is looking a little miserable and needs a treat to cheer him up!

YOU'LL NEED
(to make enough to keep your cat happy for many weeks)

- 2 lamb chops
- 1 teaspoon oil
- 100g liver, chopped into pieces
- 500ml water
- Pinch of basil
- 1 small carrot, grated
- 50g frozen peas
- 1 small potato, grated

1 Gently brown the chops and liver with the oil in a saucepan. After about five minutes, add in the water and bring to the boil. Simmer gently for about ten minutes before adding in the remaining ingredients, then continue to cook for another ten minutes.

2 Finally, fish out the chops and remove all the bone. Finely dice the cooked meat and return it to the pan. Stir well, allow to cool, and serve.

Did you know ...
that many cat foods only contain 4% meat? Just take a closer look at the ingredients next time you're shopping for pet food.

 # joe & jill's fish stew

This is an easy recipe which uses my Joe & Jill's natural cat biscuits as the main ingredient, so it's healthy as an everyday dish (as well as being really tasty!) The added fish complements the kibbles really well, and adds oily nutrients as well as extra taste.

YOU'LL NEED (to make enough for several helpings)

- 100g Joe & Jill's Fresh Salmon and Rice biscuits
- 400ml water
- 1 tin mackerel or pilchards
- ¼ teaspoon catnip (optional)

1 Put the biscuits and water into a large saucepan and bring to the boil, then let it simmer for about twenty minutes. After about ten minutes, start to mash up the softened kibbles with a wooden spoon, and keep going at it until you've formed a thick and smooth gravy. Add more water if the mixture is getting too thick.

2 Then simply mix in the mashed up fish with the catnip and let the stew cool down before serving.

treats

Everyone loves a treat – whether it's a box of chocolates with a film, or a glass of wine after a long day at work, it's nice to treat yourself every now and then as it helps you relax, unwind and feel good.

And we're not the only ones who deserve the occasional treat. Our cats have pretty stressful days too you know – chasing intruders out of the garden, digging up the roses, remembering to stretch when sleeping by the fire – it's not all plain sailing for our feline companions!

But the trouble with treats, and this is particularly true when it comes to treats for cats, is that many of them are really unhealthy, and can lead to serious health problems like obesity. So I've come up with some recipes for exciting and tasty treats for your cat that won't pile on the puss pounds. Don't go mad and feed these all the time, but a few of these treats every week will bring a smile to your cat's whiskers, without adding girth to his stomach!

 salmon pâté

This recipe is ideal as a regular treat, because it's low in fat and salt, and contains healthy protein from the salmon and egg. It was the inspiration behind Joe & Jill's Fresh Salmon and Rice diet, which contains 26% fresh salmon, making it just as healthy and nutritious as this home cooked recipe.

Make a batch of the pâté and store it in the fridge, giving a little taste every day with her dinner – or why not give half to a cat-loving friend?

YOU'LL NEED (for a good sized dish of pâté)

- 1 large (200g) can salmon
- ¼ cup breadcrumbs
- ¼ cup celery, finely chopped
- 1 egg, beaten
- 1 envelope plain gelatine
- 125ml water

1 Simply combine all the ingredients together and press firmly into a mould (ideally fish shaped, but the cat won't mind!).

2 Cook in a moderate oven for 40 minutes and turn out. Cover and allow to cool for an hour.

3 Chill in the fridge to store, but serve at room temperature with your cat's complete food. Prepare yourself for lots of contented purring and grateful leg-rubbing!

What you serve your cat's food in can affect the way it tastes – plastic bowls tend to trap old odours and tastes which can put cats off their food. The best thing to use is a ceramic or glass dish.

crunch puppets

This is one of my all-time favourites. Not only is it a tasty and healthy treat recipe – it also provides you and the cat with hours of entertainment, and even exercises the cat at the same time!

The crunchy treats are baked onto lengths of string, so you can tease the cat to your heart's content before you let him eat one. Those long winter nights will just fly past!

YOU'LL NEED

- 100g whole wheat flour
- ½ small tin tuna
- 1 dessertspoon olive oil
- 25g cheddar cheese, grated
- ½ egg
- ½ teaspoon catnip
- A ball of string

1 Firstly, cut the string into about 15 lengths of roughly 30cm each and put them into a large bowl of water. Leave them to soak for ten minutes while you prepare the biscuit dough.

2 To make the biscuit mixture, simply mix the ingredients together in a large bowl, adding a little water if required to make a firm dough. Roll this out on a floured surface, and cut into 2cm squares.

3 Now drain the water from the string and place one end of each bit of string along the middle of a square of dough, and fold the dough over to enclose the string. Then knead each folded square into a rough ball, with the string emerging from the centre.

4 Place each ball and string on a well-grease baking tray and cook for 20 minutes in a moderate oven. The moisture in the string should prevent it from charring.

5 When cooled, it's playtime! (Just make sure you keep hold of the string when he gets his teeth into the treat – string can cause a lot of trouble if swallowed!).

cheesy bacon mice

One for the cultured cat that loves the thrill of the chase, but doesn't like to get his paws dirty catching actual, real mice. These treats are crispy on the outside and full of tasty cheese and on the inside – and even feature a bacon tail!

Roll one of these across the kitchen floor and watch Puss chase after it as if it were alive and squeaking!

YOU'LL NEED (for a litter of 5 cheesy mice)

- 5 small cubes of cheese
- 5 rashers bacon
- Catnip (optional)

1 Simply place a cube of cheese at one end of a piece of bacon. Sprinkle on a little catnip if you have some, and then wrap the bacon around the cheese, tucking the last few centimetres back underneath the previous layer to secure it and leave a tail of bacon hanging from one end.

2 Place the mice on a baking tray and cook in a moderate oven (180°C/350°F/Gas 4) for about 15 minutes, by which time they should be crispy and oozing cheese. Allow to cool before rolling one across the floor and letting the games begin!

3 The mice will live quite happily in an airtight box in the fridge for a week or so, so you can ration your cat to one every few days – and don't forget to make him work for it, as they are quite rich in energy!

NUTRITION TIP

Warming your cat's food up to body temperature makes it more palatable whether it's one of these fresh recipes or their normal wet food.

tuna & marmite milkshake

Now many of the recipes in this book might sound quite tasty – but not this one! The idea of mixing fish, Marmite and milk together really makes my stomach turn – but cats (and possibly some pregnant women) think this is a dreamy combination. Just hold your nose and mix this up and watch how quickly your cat gulps it down – and if you happen to be pregnant, you never know, you might just love it!

Health-wise, it's not bad, as the tuna provides some high-quality protein and essential fatty acids, and the Marmite gives a good shot of B vitamins. There is a touch too much salt to make this an everyday treat, and cow's milk can upset some cats that don't cope well with lactose, so use this for special occasions, especially in the summer when it's great served ice cold.

YOU'LL NEED (to make one super-sized kitty shake)

- **A small can of tuna**
- **250ml milk**
- **½ teaspoon Marmite**

Simply blend it all together to form a thick milkshake. Serve slightly warmed in the winter, or straight from the fridge in the summer.

Some cats love eating grass and it's a healthy snack food. It can make them sick if they eat too much, but in general it is fine and you shouldn't discourage your cat from a little gentle grazing. If your cat is an indoor cat, why not see if she'd fancy a little dish of freshly cut grass occasionally?

chicken & catnip jelly

Jelly is the mainstay of a children's party, but it's not just kids who like the wobbly texture of jelly – some cats will go crazy for it! And rather than upsetting the children by feeding their party food to the cat, you can make up this special chicken jelly just for Puss. It's much healthier than the sweet variety the kids love, and the taste is more suited to the feline palate than raspberry or lemon!

This recipe makes a pint of jelly – enough for a whole party of cats – so halve the quantities if you've just got one or two cats:

YOU'LL NEED (to make a pint of jelly)

- 1 chicken drumstick
- 1 small carrot
- 1 stock cube
- ½ teaspoon catnip
- 1 tablespoon gelatine

1   Boil up the chicken and chopped carrot in enough water to comfortably cover them. Add in the stock cube and simmer for about half an hour, and then remove the carrot and chicken from the water and put them to one side.

2   Pour about 100ml of the broth into a mixing bowl and add in the gelatine, mix thoroughly and then top up to 450ml with the broth, and add the catnip.

3   Then allow the mixture to cool before pouring a little into the bottom of a suitable mould (a giant mouse perhaps?) Put the mould into the fridge and wait for it to start to set (this may take an hour or more). Then add in a few small pieces of chicken meat from the drumstick, and cover with another layer of jelly liquid. Repeat this, allowing the jelly to set as you go, until you have filled the mould(s) and used up all the meat.

4   Put back in the fridge to set completely and just remember not to confuse it with the children's jelly at the party!

Did you know ...
that cats are obligate carnivores which means they have to eat meat and can't survive on a vegetarian diet?

fishy frozen yoghurt

This is the ideal summertime cat treat – and it's pretty good health-wise too. Yoghurt is basically milk that has had the sugar converted to lactic acid by bacteria, and it's these bacteria which give yoghurt its healthy properties.

It's full of calcium for strong bones, good quality protein, and vitamins A and B. Combine this with the health-giving properties of oily fish like sardines, and you have a treat that will keep your cat cool, satisfied and in tiptop condition in the summer!

YOU'LL NEED

- 1 large (450g) pot of live plain yoghurt
- 1 tin sardines

1   Simply mash up the sardines with a fork and mix them into the yoghurt in a large bowl – whiz up with a blender if you want, or just keep mixing with a fork until reasonably smooth. Then pour into paper cupcakes and put them on a tray in the freezer.

2   To serve, simply remove one from the freezer, pop it out of its paper case, and drop it into Puss' bowl.

kitten food

Bringing up a little kitten is a great experience – except perhaps for those moments when he demolishes the potted plants or shreds the sofa cushions - but looking after the little ball of trouble takes a bit of thinking about, with visits to the vet for vaccinations, and worming to fit in, as well as making sure he eats a proper, healthy diet.

The best food for your kitten is a good quality complete food containing just the right mix of nutrients your kitten needs to grow up big and strong – but that doesn't mean there's no room for a bit of home cooking in your kitten's life. These recipes are a wonderful way of giving your new friend a healthy treat every now and then – and you never know, he might even leave the curtains alone for a while as a thank you!

 kitten smoothie

There are lots of recipes around for suitable milk-replacement drinks for kittens, but from my experience, this is the best one. It's ideal for sickly kittens that aren't eating, or young kittens orphaned by their mother – or just as a tasty treat for the older kitten!

YOU'LL NEED

- 300ml water
- 1 envelope gelatine
- 1 can whole evaporated milk
- 2 tablespoons mayonnaise
- 2 tablespoons plain yoghurt

1   Boil up the water and add the gelatine, stirring well. Then take off the heat and add the rest of the ingredients, continuing to stir as you do so. Then let the mixture cool down and store in the fridge, where it will set to form a thick sludge.

2   Warm up as much as you need to room temperature to serve, and the rest will keep in the fridge for 2 weeks. Alternatively you can freeze it in an ice cube tray and defrost it cube by cube as required.

kitten's breakfast

We all love starting the day with a good cooked breakfast, so why not treat your kitten to a nutritious snack in the morning? This recipe for fishy scrambled eggs is both tasty and healthy, and can be fed as often as you like. It's also fine for older cats, and I've known a few who have never lost their taste for this dish and have eaten it regularly throughout their lives.

YOU'LL NEED (to make enough for a couple of kittens)

- 2 eggs
- Butter
- 1 tablespoon milk
- 1 small tin salmon
- 1 tablespoon mayonnaise

Scramble the eggs in a saucepan with a small knob of butter and the milk. Cook over a gentle heat, mixing continuously until the egg mixture is fluffy and cooked through. Remove from the heat and mash in the fish and then add the mayonnaise. Mix it all together and serve once it's cooled to room temperature.

🐾 kitten cheesy treats

I initially developed this recipe for puppies as a treat to help with training – but when Jill kept following me around, picking up the crumbs and meowing, I realised that they are just as popular with cats. I've tweaked the recipe a little from the puppy biscuits, and also added in some catnip just to make cats really go wild for them, and now they are guaranteed to appeal to just about any cat.

They're ideal for treating your new kitten (or older cat) whenever she does something good – or just if you want to give her something nice every now and then. But be careful not to give more than one or two a day, as they are fattening and you don't want to let your kitten get overweight.

YOU'LL NEED (for enough to keep your kitten happy for months)

- 125g whole wheat flour
- 75g cheddar cheese, grated
- 25g butter
- 1 teaspoon catnip
- Milk

1 Mix the flour and butter together in a large bowl and run the fat in until it forms a crumbly mixture. Then add in the grated cheese and catnip and mix well.

2 Slowly add milk to the mixture until it forms a very sticky dough. Flour your hands and start kneading the dough until it forms a single firm lump. Then turn it out onto a floured surface and roll it out to about ¼ inch thick. Score the dough with a sharp knife to form tiny squares which you can break apart once it's cooked.

3 Then place the rolled and scored dough onto a greased baking tray and cook in a moderate oven (180°C/350F/Gas 4) for 15–20 minutes, until it's golden brown. Allow to cool and then break up into the little squares along your score lines. Store in an airtight container and they'll keep for several weeks.

Did you know ...
that dogs can safely eat cat food but cats shouldn't eat dog food as it doesn't meet their needs?

kitten food

 # baby beef balls

Apparently lots of people own pets because they're a baby substitute. So here's a recipe which uses proper baby food to make a delicious treat for your kitten!

Make them round and you can roll them around the floor and get the kitten to chase them – this will keep her happy for hours, and give your curtains and ornaments a rest from her troublesome attentions…

YOU'LL NEED

- 100g plain flour
- 1 tablespoon milk
- 1 teaspoon honey
- 1 small jar of beef baby food

1   Mix the flour, honey and baby food together in a small bowl until they form a gooey paste. Then add the milk, a little at a time, until you can knead the mixture into a dough.

2   Then form the dough into small balls and place them on a greased baking tray. Bake for about ten minutes in a moderate oven and allow to cool before rolling one across the floor and watching the kitten scrabbling wildly after it!

3 Store in an airtight container in the fridge for up to a week – and bring out whenever you need to distract the kitten from causing trouble!

NUTRITION TIP

Think about where your cat's food comes from – if it's a complete food, has it been made overseas and flown thousands of miles to reach your cat's dish? And if you're using fresh ingredients for one of these recipes, think about using locally grown produce where possible to save on those air miles – even cats have a carbon paw print!

creamy liver delight

As a way of giving your kitten a really good dose of vitamins and minerals there's little to beat a meal of liver. This recipe uses cooked liver and combines it with fresh cream to make a really thick and nutritious kitten treat. This is a recipe to be used only occasionally as it is so rich; however much your kitten begs for more, it's a once-a-week-at-most treat!

YOU'LL NEED (for a couple of hungry kttens)

- 100g chicken liver
- 1 tablespoon single cream
- 1 tablespoon plain yoghurt

1 All you need to do is cover the liver in boiling water and let it stand for ten minutes to cook.

2 Then blend the liver, cream and yoghurt together until it forms a creamy milkshake-like mixture that you can pour into the kitten's bowls once cooled to room temperature.

meals for special occasions

Our feline friends give us an awful lot of pleasure –
a friendly cuddle on the sofa, a cheery meow in the
morning (not mentioning of course the hair on the
best furniture and mice in the kitchen, but that's another
story...) so it's nice to be able to give them something back
once in a while. Here are a few recipes for those special
days in your cat's life, when you want to say 'thank you'
with a really memorable meal.

 birthday cake

What better way to celebrate the cat's big day than with a big, fishy cake? You might think this is a bit extravagant, but if you've got the time, why not make a real fuss on her special day?

This recipe is based on my dog birthday cake, but with some important changes. For a start I use chicken mince instead of beef, as I think most cats prefer it, and I've replaced the carrot with some fish paste, just to add a little extra taste. A sprinkling of catnip is the final addition – guaranteed to appeal to even the fussiest of birthday cats!

YOU'LL NEED (to make a cake big enough for 3 or 4 cats)

- 200g chicken mince
- 75g oatmeal
- 75g plain flour
- 30g butter
- 2 eggs
- 1 jar fish paste
- Yoghurt
- 1 teaspoon catnip

1. Fry the mince until brown. Meanwhile, mix together the flour and oatmeal and rub in the butter. Beat in the eggs to form a sticky paste, and then add in the mince and fish paste, complete with any juice from the pan. Knead the mixture together and press it into a well-greased cake tin. Cook for 30 minutes in a moderate oven and then turn out and allow to cool.

2. Cover the cake with yoghurt and sprinkle on the catnip. Candles are an optional extra but don't expect your cat to blow them out as you sing 'Happy Birthday' and do remove them before you have a set of singed whiskers on your hands!

NUTRITION TIP

Cats know what's good for them and will often turn their whiskers up at foods containing poor quality ingredients – so to keep your cat happy and healthy, make sure you feed them a top-quality diet!

marmite cheesecake

This is another cake recipe for those feline special occasions – first day at the cattery, fathering a litter, not destroying the flowerbeds for a whole month – any excuse to get in the kitchen and treat your cat to something mouth-wateringly tasty.

And the good news is that this recipe won't turn your sleek puss into a fat cat overnight – it uses low fat ingredients and her own dried food for the base – so you can bake it and feed a little bit every day until it's finished up.

YOU'LL NEED (to make the base)

- **50g dried cat food**
- **20g butter or margarine**
- **25g plain flour**

1   To make the biscuit base, first (carefully!) pulverise the cat food by wrapping it in an old tea towel and hitting it with a rolling pin. Alternatively you can use a blender which is easier – but nowhere near as much fun! Then add just enough warm water to make it into a really moist and gooey mess. Leave it to stand for ten minutes, and add more water if you need to, as the kibble absorbs a lot of water.

2 Then add in the flour and butter, and mix it all together to form a thick dough. It should form up into a nice dry ball that you can roll out on a floured surface until it's about ¼ inch thick. Press this into the bottom of a greased cheesecake tin.

YOU'LL NEED (to make the cheesy topping)

- 2 egg whites
- 1 tablespoon sugar
- 1 tablespoon cornflour
- 1½ cups low-fat cottage cheese
- 1 teaspoon Marmite

3 For the topping, simply add all the ingredients into a blender and whiz them up until they are really smooth. Then pour over the base to fill the tin, and cook in a low oven (160°C/325°F/Gas3) for an hour. Chill in the fridge before serving.

🐾 pussy cat pizza

'Pizza for cats?' I hear you cry. 'What a silly idea!' Well, you can be forgiven for thinking that pizza is not exactly an ideal meal for the average cat – but there again, this is not exactly your average pizza. Made with a healthy cat-food based base, and topped with fish, this is a new twist on the Italian pizza tradition, specifically designed for the more adventurous feline palate (in other words, not all cats will like this!).

YOU'LL NEED

- 50g dried cat food
- 25g plain flour
- 20g butter or margarine
- 1 teaspoon catnip
- 1 tin oily fish – mackerel, sardines or pilchards – in tomato sauce
- 30g Cheddar cheese, grated

1 This bit is about as much fun as you can have in the kitchen – take small handfuls of the cat kibble, wrap it up in an old tea towel, and bash it to bits with a rolling pin. Keep this up until you've reduced all the kibble to a fine powder. Just watch your fingers because, believe me, it hurts when you wallop them with the rolling pin! (As with the cheesecake, you can use a blender – but it's much less enjoyable!).

2 Next, moisten the kibble powder with enough warm water to make it into a really moist and gooey mess. Leave it to stand for ten minutes, and add more water if you need to, as the kibble absorbs a lot of water. Then add in the flour and butter, and mix it all together until it's a thick dough. It should form up into a nice dry ball which you can roll out on a floured surface until it's about ¼ inch thick.

3 For the topping, spread the fish in tomato sauce over the base and sprinkle on the grated cheese and catnip.

4 Cook in a moderate oven for 20–25 minutes – until the top is golden brown. Allow to cool thoroughly and then slice into wedges before serving.

a heart for valentine's day

If the 14th February comes around and you find yourself all alone with no-one to share the romantic day with, you could do worse than cook up this tasty meal for your cat. After all, the cat won't disappoint by not turning up, or make excuses and leave early, and he's guaranteed to listen as you pour your feelings out.

So, cook up this meal, order yourself a takeaway, open some wine, and cuddle up with the contented cat on the sofa and watch a romantic film on the box. Who needs a real Valentine's date anyway!

YOU'LL NEED

- 200g beef heart
- 50g liver
- 1 tablespoon oil
- 50g spinach, finely chopped
- 1 tablespoon carrot, finely grated
- 2 eggs
- 50g rice

1 Boil the heart for about fifteen minutes, then add the liver to the pan and continue to cook for another five minutes. Drain and cut up the heart and liver into dice-sized pieces.

2   Gently cook the carrot in the oil before adding in the spinach and cooking for a few minutes – until it has reduced down. Meanwhile, boil the rice and drain when cooked, and beat the eggs together in a mixing bowl.

3   Add the heart, liver, rice, and carrot and spinach to the egg mixture and combine thoroughly. Then return to the frying pan and cook, stirring continuously until the eggs are cooked. Cool and serve with a romantic sigh...

Did you know ...

that a condition called hyperthyroidism can make cats very hungry and lose weight? Thankfully it's easy to treat!

special occasions

Many cats don't like tap water because of the taste of chlorine. If your cat doesn't seem to be drinking the water you put down then offer rain water or bottled water instead.

# Christmas turkey & fish stroganoff

Cats are well-known for being the world's pickiest food snobs – offer them something not quite to their taste and they'll turn up their whiskers with a disdainful meow. So trying to offer your cat a special meal at Christmas that's both healthy and tasty requires a little thought – which is where I've been busy on your behalf! This easy recipe is guaranteed to appeal to the fussiest of cats, and is full of healthy goodness so they won't be in need of a Boxing Day diet!

YOU'LL NEED (to make enough for one cat)

- A handful of crumbled turkey breast from your leftover roast
- 1 teaspoon of fish paste
- ½ teaspoon cranberry sauce
- 1 dessertspoon of single cream
- ¼ teaspoon Marmite (or similar yeast extract)

1 Simply mix all of the ingredients together in a small bowl to form a creamy paste with small chunks of turkey meat. Serve with a side order of healthy natural dried food and your cat will enjoy a Christmas meal to rival yours (although don't compare the two – the cat will love this recipe but you won't!).

 Easter rabbit

With the coming of spring, rabbits will undoubtedly be on your cat's mind – and quite possibly in his mouth if he gets half a chance. This delicious rabbit recipe is the ideal way to satisfy his springtime urge for rabbit, without having to put up with a half-dead animal being dragged in through the cat flap and deposited proudly on the living room carpet!

This makes enough to keep even the most rabbit-crazy cat satisfied for several weeks.

YOU'LL NEED (makes approximately 10 burgers)

- 1 small rabbit, quartered
- 3 slices of bacon, cut into thirds
- 1 carrot, grated
- 3 tablespoons plain flour
- 300ml beef stock (from stock cube if you don't have fresh)
- 1 teaspoon dried thyme
- 2 teaspoons dried parsley
- 1 teaspoon dried catnip

1 Fry the bacon for a few minutes until cooked, remove from the pan and set aside for another use (bacon salad? A nice bacon sarnie?). Then cook the grated carrot in the bacon fat left behind – for extra flavour – before adding in the rabbit pieces. Continue to fry until the rabbit is golden brown. Then sprinkle on the flour to cover the rabbit and continue to cook for another five minutes or so.

2 Add in the beef stock and herbs and simmer for about an hour. Allow to cool completely and remove all the bones (very important to get all of them out, otherwise you could be spending Easter Monday at the vet).

3 Serve with some rice or mashed potatoes, and store what you don't use in the fridge for up to 5 days, or the freezer for a few months.

🐾 nine-life nosh

This is a really special recipe designed to restore your cat to full health after he's survived a particularly close call and used up one of his nine lives. So maybe he's just recovered after an accident, or had an operation – or just scraped an escape from the Rottweiller next door. Whatever the occasion, this feast of 9 different sources of protein will get him back on track and restore him back to a full set of nine lives.

YOU'LL NEED

- 1 small piece of chicken breast, diced
- 1 small strip of stewing steak, diced
- 1 rasher bacon
- 1 small piece liver, chopped
- 1 lamb's kidney, sliced
- ¼ tin of sardines
- 100g spinach
- 1 slice ham
- 1 small slice black pudding, cooked
- ¼ hardboiled egg

1 Fry the bacon, steak and chicken together, adding a little oil if necessary. Cook gently until all the pieces are browned and then add in the chopped liver and kidney and continue to cook for another five or six minutes. Finally, add the spinach and cook until reduced.

2   Then remove from the heat and mix in the tin of sardines, complete with oil. Cut up the ham and add to the mixture, and then mash in the cooked black pudding and hardboiled egg. Finally, grind up some of the egg shell as finely as you can and sprinkle ½ teaspoon of the powder into the mix, just to add a little extra calcium.

3   Serve and watch your cat magically re-grow his lost life – or alternatively he might just meow happily and trot off for a nap on the sofa!

4   This is ideal to freeze, so you can have a portion on hand for next time the cat gets rescued from a tree, or falls out of the bedroom window!

NUTRITION TIP

One of the reasons that cats need to eat meat is that they can't make their own vitamin A (unlike dogs), and need to get this essential vitamin from their diet. As plants don't contain vitamin A, cats have to eat meat in order to stay healthy.

pilchards & popcorn

If you're having a night in with a film, and cooking up a little popcorn to keep you going, why not put a little aside for the cat and make up this cheeky little recipe for her. It'll keep her busy in the kitchen while you can relax with the film – or until she comes back through to thank you with a fishy purr …

YOU'LL NEED

- **A handful of cooked popcorn**
- **½ tin pilchards in oil**
- **½ teaspoon catnip** (optional)

1   So, while the trailers are on, just mix together the popcorn and pilchards (and catnip if you have some) and set it down for the cat.

2   The interesting texture and taste combination will keep her amused for at least the first half hour of the film, and fill her up so she doesn't pester you at the dramatic finale!

special occasions

meals to share

There are times when you have to face the fact that it's just you and cat for the evening. The other half's out, your friends are busy, and there's a long evening stretching ahead. So what better than to cook yourself a lovely meal that you can share with your one loyal friend (assuming, that is, he hasn't just disappeared out of the cat flap!).

These recipes are specially designed to be tasty and healthy for both of you, so you can enjoy them together – just keep the wine to yourself!

🐾 haddock & coriander fish cakes with rice

Now those of you who've also got dogs, and have a copy of my dog recipe book will find this recipe very familiar. In fact it's pretty much identical to the recipe I made for dogs and their owners, because I quickly realised (with a little help from Jill) that cats love these fish cakes just as much as dogs do.

YOU'LL NEED (to make enough for 2 people and a cat)

- 500g potatoes
- 250g haddock fillet
- 150ml milk
- 1 egg, beaten
- 2 tablespoons coriander, chopped
- 40g breadcrumbs
- 1 tablespoon oil

1 Boil the peeled potatoes for about 15 minutes, until they are nice and soft. Meanwhile put the fish in a large saucepan and cover with the milk. Bring to the boil and then immediately turn off the heat and allow to cook on its own for 5 minutes, by which time it should be nice and flaky. Remove from the milk and discard any skin and bones.

2 Mash the potatoes and add in the coriander and the flaked fish. Mix well and form into 8 cakes. Dip each cake in the beaten egg and coat with breadcrumbs. Heat the oil in a frying pan and cook the cakes for about 7–8 minutes, turning halfway through. Drain with kitchen paper to absorb the oil and serve with rice and veg for you, and Joe & Jill's Fresh Salmon and Rice for Puss!

NUTRITION TIP

Cats don't need carbohydrates in their food. It's included in most pet foods because it's a cheap source of energy, but in the wild, cats would get their energy from fat and protein.

chicken stroganoff

Cats love cream, and this recipe will tickle their taste buds as much as it does yours. It isn't a super-healthy meal, as the cream and butter adds quite a lot of fat but, as with most things, in moderation it's fine for both you and the cat. Just make sure you and the cat get a bit of exercise to earn this dinner, so arm yourself with a ball of string and a ball of paper and work up an appetite for you both!

One other thing to note about this recipe is the fact that it has both mushrooms and onions in, neither of which is ideal for cats – so remember to follow the last part of the instructions, and just feed the chicken and sauce to the cat.

YOU'LL NEED (for you, a friend, and the cat)

- 450g chicken breasts, cut into slices
- 1 onion, chopped coarsely
- 200g mushrooms, sliced
- 100g plain flour
- ½ teaspoon salt
- ½ teaspoon pepper
- 3 tablespoons butter
- 1 teaspoon mustard
- 1 teaspoon paprika
- 150ml chicken stock
- 75ml sour cream
- 75ml plain yoghurt
- 200g rice

1. Set the rice going by adding to a large pan of boiling water and simmering as per the instructions on the packet.

2. Meanwhile, mix together the flour, salt and pepper and roll in the chicken until it is nicely coated. Then melt the butter in a frying pan and cook the chicken until light golden in colour. Add in the onion and mushrooms and cook for a further five minutes.

3. Then mix in the mustard, paprika and chicken stock. Cover and simmer for another five minutes before adding the sour cream and yoghurt. Cook for a final 2 minutes before taking off the heat and serving with the rice (which you've previously drained when just tender).

4. For the cat, pick out a couple of nice-looking pieces of chicken and serve on a bed of rice and cover with a spoonful of sauce, without any onion or mushroom if possible.

fish, chips 'n' mushy peas

There're few things better than good old fish and chips – but the trouble is it's not exactly what you'd call a healthy meal option. All those saturated fats from the fryer add taste but are also rather good at gumming up your arteries and adding to your waistline. And while our feline friends might be partial to a nibble from your chip shop's best, it won't do him many favours in the health department either.

So here is a recipe that means both you and your cat can enjoy a dinner of fish and chips, but avoid the fats associated with the deep fat fryer. This recipe is full of the natural unsaturated fats from the fish, including the excellent omega-3 oils which are good for your heart (and the cat's), as well as providing carbohydrate and fibre from the sweet potato chips and vitamins from the mushy peas.

YOU'LL NEED (to feed 2 people and a hungry cat)

- 2 large cod, plaice or halibut fillets
- 60g breadcrumbs
- Zest and juice of 2 limes
- 1 tablespoon fresh parsley
- 500g sweet potatoes
- 2 tablespoons olive oil
- 1 tin mushy peas

1. Slice up the sweet potatoes into wedge-shaped chips and put them in a roasting tin. Pour over the olive oil, shake to make sure they're completely covered, and put them in a moderate oven to start cooking.

2. Meanwhile, mix together the breadcrumbs, lime zest and juice and parsley, and press into the fish to cover as completely as possible. Then take the potatoes out of the oven, clear a space in the centre, and place the fish in the tin. Return to the oven and cook for 30 minutes, turning the fish once. When the fish and chips are nearly done, heat up the peas in the microwave.

3. Break off a little from each fish fillet once they're cooked and set aside along with one or two chips and a teaspoon of peas to cool down for the cat. Eat yours, and then serve the cat's mashed up with a dab of tartar sauce.

peking duck noodles

I must admit to having 'borrowed' this recipe from a normal cook book, but after a friend's cat demolished a plate full at a dinner party recently, I knew I had to include it – and what a treat this recipe is for both you and the cat. There's nothing cats like more than duck meat, with its rich gamey flavour and fatty juices, and add in the fun of chasing noodles around the kitchen floor and this is a sure fire winner all round!

YOU'LL NEED (to feed a family and a cat)

- 1 duck – around 2kg
- 1 tablespoon dark muscovado sugar
- 1 teaspoon salt
- 1 large packet noodles (around 250g)
- 1 tablespoon olive oil
- 1 inch piece of fresh root ginger, peeled and diced
- 1 vegetable stock cube dissolved in 600ml boiling water
- 1 tablespoon cornflour mixed with a little water
- 1 tablespoon sweet chilli sauce (optional, depending on your cat's taste for chillies!)
- 1 tablespoon soy sauce
- 4 Chinese leaves, shredded
- 4 spring onions, thinly sliced
- Handful of basil leaves to serve

1. Soften the duck by piercing it with a skewer 4 or 5 times, and then pouring over a kettle-full of boiling water while it stands on a rack over a roasting dish. Drain away the water and rub in the sugar and salt mixed together. Leave the duck in a cool, dry place for about 2 hours.

2. Then preheat the oven to (200°C/400°F/Gas 6) and roast the duck for 1½ hours basting occasionally, until the skin is crisp and dark, and the meat cooked through. Leave to stand for 10 minutes.

3. While the duck is standing, cook the noodles by covering them in boiling water in a bowl and leaving them for 2 minutes before draining. Then heat the oil in a wok and add in the noodles and ginger. Cook for 3 minutes without stirring so the noodles at the bottom crisp up. Then stir to loosen up the noodles, and add in the vegetable stock, cornflour, chilli sauce, soy sauce, Chinese leaves, and spring onions and stir fry for 2–3 minutes.

4. Break away the duck meat using a knife and serve each portion of noodles with several piece of duck meat on top. Garnish with basil leaves.

For the cat, pick out the spring onion if you can, as this isn't wonderful for cats, and serve his portion with the meat mashed together with the noodles.

eggs with anchovies

This is a cracking recipe for a starter, which goes down just as well with the cat as it does with the guests at a dinner party. The protein from the eggs, and essential oils from the fish make this really healthy – and of course any self-respecting cat will go wild for the strong taste of anchovies. I've left out the garlic which is in the original recipe for this dish, and added in some fromage frais to reduce the fat content for the cat, but otherwise it's just how you'd cook it for yourself.

YOU'LL NEED (for a small dinner party and a medium-sized cat)

- 1 tin of anchovies in oil, drained
- ¼ teaspoon dried thyme
- ½ teaspoon Dijon mustard
- 1½ tablespoons red wine vinegar
- Freshly ground black pepper
- 100ml olive oil
- 5 hardboiled eggs
- Fromage frais

1 Mix together all of the ingredients, except the oil, eggs and fromage frais, in a blender and purée for about 1 minute. Then, with the blender running, slowly add the oil in the thin stream and blend until thick and smooth.

2. Serve each egg with a drizzle of the anchovy sauce and store the rest in the fridge. For the cat's portion, break up the egg with a fork, and mash together with ½ teaspoon of the sauce and a teaspoon of fromage frais. This prevents the dish being too fatty for your cat, as this could cause problems like pancreatitis.

Did you know ...
that raw eggs can cause a dietary deficiency and lead to skin disease?

❤️ creamy pasta with chicken & spinach

This is an ideal recipe for those evenings when you're late home from work and just want to throw something together that's easy and tasty – and that also satisfies the cat, who's been meowing around your feet ever since you got in!

YOU'LL NEED (to make enough for you and the cat)

- **200g pasta**
  (any shape will do)
- **1 teaspoon olive oil**
- **100g chicken breast, cooked**
- **150ml fromage frais**
- **100g shredded spinach**
- **50g Parmesan cheese, flaked**

1. Cook the pasta in a large pan of boiling water until just tender. Drain and return to the pan.

2. Meanwhile, break the chicken into small pieces and gently fry in the oil for five minutes until crispy and brown. Add in the shredded spinach and continue cooking for a couple of minutes until it has reduced down. Then pour in the fromage frais and cook until the sauce is hot through.

3 Pour the chicken sauce over the pasta, add half the Parmesan and toss to mix thoroughly. Sprinkle on the remaining Parmesan and serve – hot for you and cold for the cat.

NUTRITION TIP

Cats prefer salty, sour and bitter tastes to sweet flavours, so remember this when you're inventing your own feline feast if you want it to go down well!

macaroni cheese

Not an obvious choice for a cat-friendly meal you might think, but most cats love anything cheesy and this simple macaroni recipe is great for you as well as the cat. Mix her portion with a touch of Marmite if she prefers, just for bit of extra taste, or stir in some tinned cat food (just remember to separate off your portion first…).

YOU'LL NEED (to make a family-sized dish full)

- 250g macaroni
- 120g cheddar cheese
- 450ml milk
- 40g plain flour
- 40g butter
- 1 teaspoon wholegrain mustard
- Marmite to taste (for the cat)

1 Cook the pasta according to the instructions on the packet. Meanwhile, make the cheese sauce by melting the butter in a saucepan over a low heat and stirring in the flour. Cook gently for 2–3 minutes and then add the mustard and remove from the heat. Now gradually add the milk, stirring constantly to avoid lumps. Return to the heat and bring to the boil still stirring, and simmer for 5 minutes, stirring occasionally. When smooth and creamy, stir in most of the cheese a little at a time until melted.

2   Put the pasta into a suitable ovenproof dish, pour over
    the cheese sauce and sprinkle the remaining cheese on top.
    Cook in a moderate oven for 40 minutes, until brown and
    crisp on top.

3   Allow to cool fully before giving the cat her portion, and
    add in a dab of Marmite if she likes.

Did you know ...
that cats don't have a 'sweet tooth' because they can't taste
simple sugars such as glucose?

🐾 fish soup

Why cats like fish so much is one of those mysteries of life – I mean, how many wild cats would have gone fishing in prehistoric times? I somehow can't imagine an ancient wild cat plucking salmon out of a swirling river like a Grizzly Bear, but modern cats have certainly developed an appetite for fish from somewhere.

But wherever their taste for fish came from, there's no denying the fact that most cats can't get enough it, and this recipe is fishy enough to go down a storm with most feline-fish-fanciers – and what's more, it's delicious for you as well.

YOU'LL NEED (for a large pot full, which will keep you and the cat going all week)

- 4 carrots, cut into fine strips
- 100g broccoli, finely chopped
- 100g cabbage, finely chopped
- 1 fennel bulb, finely chopped
- 1 tablespoon olive oil
- 2 litres fish stock*
- 1 ½ kg of assorted fish and shellfish**

* To make the fish stock, ask your local fishmonger for some leftover fishy bits – heads, bones, tails etc – and then boil them up in plenty of water for an hour or so to make the stock. You can cheat and use fish sauce diluted with water, but it's not quite the same!

** Try to get a real mix of fish and shellfish, with a few large pieces of fish and lots of different shellfish and smaller fish.

1. Make the soup in a large saucepan. Firstly, fry the fish pieces individually in the oil for a couple of minutes each to brown them off. Then do the same with the veg, using the same oil, before adding in the shellfish and returning the cooked fish to the pan. Pour in the stock and bring to the boil.

2. Simmer for about 15 minutes and serve immediately (for you – wait until it's cooled for the cat).

poached salmon linguine

This is such a simple recipe, rich in flavour, that appeals just as much to your cat as it does to you. The poached salmon is about as healthy a protein source as you can get, and the pasta provides a great source of good quality carbohydrate – to keep you going at the gym, and Puss full of energy for his nightly patrols of the garden!

YOU'LL NEED (feeds two plus the cat)

- 400g salmon fillet cut into three pieces
- ½ lemon, peeled and thinly sliced
- 1 teaspoon tarragon, chopped
- ½ teaspoon fresh black pepper
- ½ teaspoon sea salt
- 100ml olive oil
- 300g dried linguine
- 50g sun dried tomatoes
- 50g wild rocket

1 Place the salmon in a shallow baking dish and put the lemon slices on top. Sprinkle on the tarragon, pepper and salt and pour over the olive oil. Cook for 30 minutes in a cool oven (150°C/300°F/Gas 2).

2 Meanwhile, cook the pasta in a large pan of boiling water until tender but still firm. Drain and return to the pan.

3 Take the salmon out of the oil and break into the pasta in large flakes. Add 1 tablespoon of the olive oil from the pan together with the lemon and rocket and mix well. Divide off a small portion for the cat and set to one side. Then add the tomatoes to the remainder and mix again before serving for yourselves. Let the cat loose on his once it has thoroughly cooled.

NUTRITION TIP

Some cats won't eat if there's too much noise around so feed them somewhere quiet so they can have a nice relaxed dinner for one!

meals for older cats

As your cat gets older, his nutritional needs will change, and the recipes you cook for him will have to meet his new requirements. For example, as a young, active cat, he would be burning off far more calories than he does now, so he needs less energy in his food. And then there's his sense of smell – where it used to be sensitive enough to smell out a home cooked meal at half a mile, now he needs strong tastes and flavours to attract him and whet his appetite.

These recipes are designed with the healthy older cat in mind, and are not necessarily ideal for older cats with health problems, such as kidney failure or diabetes – these conditions are catered for in the final section of the book. So when your cat enters middle age (8–10 years old), and he's got a clean bill of health from your vet, treat to him to one of these healthy and strong tasting recipes once in a while to perk him up!

 # fishy rice

Fish is a good source of easily digestible protein for older cats, and it also supplies the healthy fatty acids found in omega-3 fish oils. The addition of the anchovies in this recipe adds more oily fish as well as a really strong taste which is vital to get an older cat eating properly.

Rice is also easy to digest, and is not as rich as some other carbohydrates such as oats, which might be a little too much for an older cat. The final health-giving ingredient I've included is puréed carrot – raw veg is great for supplying natural antioxidants that help delay the onset of old age diseases such as cancer.

This recipe can be fed once a week as a healthy treat.

YOU'LL NEED

- **Small fillet of white fish**
- **½ tin anchovies**
- **50g rice**
- **½ carrot**

1   Boil the rice in a large pan of water, and steam the fish above if you have a suitable two-layered steaming pan. Otherwise cook them separately, for about 10 minutes each (until the rice is just tender).

2   Drain away the water, mix the steamed fish and rice together, and mash in the anchovies. Finally, puree the carrot in a blender, or grate it as finely as possible and then crush with a rolling pin (important to break open the cells and let the cat digest the nutrients inside). Mix in the carrot and serve. You can keep this in the fridge for about 5 days.

NUTRITION TIP

Without the essential amino acid, taurine, cats suffer from eye and heart problems and need to have a supply of this building block of protein in their diet every day.

 rabbit risotto

Just because your cat is getting older doesn't mean she doesn't still deserve the occasional real gourmet treat. This Italian-based rice recipe is an ideal meal, perhaps for her tenth birthday, or for a celebration of an all-clear from the vet after her old age blood tests.

The combination of tender rabbit – another great low-fat protein source – with soft rice and a vegetable-rich broth makes this both irresistibly tasty and healthy.

YOU'LL NEED (makes several servings)

- 100g rice
- ½ rabbit, divided into pieces
- A little olive oil
- 1 small carrot
- 1 small parsnip
- 1 stick celery

1 First, fry the rabbit for five minutes in a little olive oil, until browned all over. Then pour in enough water to comfortably cover the rabbit, and add in the chopped up veg. Bring to the boil and simmer for 30 minutes, before removing the rabbit and setting aside to cool. Mash up the veg – removing any stubborn pieces of celery – to make a rich broth.

2 Remove all the bones from the rabbit and discard them (somewhere where the cat can't get to them!) and break up the meat into small pieces.

3 Now, fry the rice gently for a few minutes in a little more oil, until it is well coated. Then pour in about 100ml of the broth, which should soak the rice without completely covering it. Turn down the heat so the liquid is just simmering, and stir as it cooks. As soon as the liquid had been absorbed, add another 100ml of broth – and keep doing this, stirring as you go – until the rice is almost cooked. Then add in the rabbit meat and keep cooking until the rice is done – it doesn't matter if it's a little sloppier than you'd like, as this is fine for cats.

4 Serve once cooled and store in the fridge for a few days – or freeze if you have lots left over.

 # fish gravy

If your elderly cat has started turning up his nose at his dinner, it could be because his sense of smell is fading. Without strong signals from his nose that something smells nice, he won't be stimulated to eat, and this could lead to a worrying loss of condition.

This gravy recipe is an ideal way of adding some extra taste to his normal dried biscuits. The strong fishy flavours are ideal for getting him interested in food again – and the recipe also adds in healthy protein and vitamins which will help him stay in good shape.

YOU'LL NEED (for a two-dog omelette)

- 450g or thereabouts of fishy remains – ask your fishmonger for leftover head, tails or bones
- 50g butter
- 2 tablespoons plain flour

1 Dice the carrot and potato and boil them for about 7–8 Place the fishy leftovers in a large saucepan and cover with water. Bring to the boil and simmer for about 40 minutes. Remove any bones and set the broth to one side.

2 Next, gently melt the butter in a pan and add the flour, cooking gently for a few minutes. Then gradually add about a pint (450ml) of the fish broth, stirring continuously until it thickens. Cook for a further 5 minutes and then take off the heat and allow to cool.

3 Keep it in the fridge, and pour a little over his dinner every day. You can also pour it into an ice-cube tray to freeze it, and then defrost one at a time (just don't forget and put one of these ice cubes in your drink – fishy G & T is not to be recommended!).

Did you know ...
that wild cats rarely drink water, because their fluid comes from their prey?

turkey & pilchard pasta

This recipe is all about taste and texture. The strong flavours of the pilchards combined with the chewy texture of al denté pasta make this dish go down really well with older cats. It's another recipe rich in healthy fish oils, which is great news if your cat is starting to feel the effects of a little arthritis in his joints.

YOU'LL NEED (to feed a couple of hungry kitties)

- 100g pasta
- 1 tin pilchards
- 50g fromage frais
- 1 tablespoon cheese, grated

1   Cook the pasta in boiling water until it is just tender – err on the side of undercooked here, as it will give the meal more texture, which cats love (it reminds them of chewing mice!).

2   Then simply mix in the pilchards, fromage frais and cheese and blend it all together until it forms a thick, fishy paste.

3   Garnish with a sprinkling of catnip if you fancy.

When you're cooking for your cat remember to 'think cat' and don't worry about how the meal tastes or smells to you – cats have a very different idea from us of what's nice and tasty!

lamb's liver smoothie

Smoothies are all the rage for people – you can get them in all sorts of flavours from mango to passion fruit – and they are the ultimate in healthy drinking. But as far as I know there aren't too many cat-friendly smoothies on the market – which is why I decided to come up with my own! This smoothie recipe uses chicken liver which is a very concentrated source of all sorts of vitamins and other goodness, so it's a great tonic to revitalise the older cat every now and then.

YOU'LL NEED (for a couple of portions)

- 50g lamb's liver, cut into small pieces
- 125ml milk
- ½ banana

1 All you need to do is cook the liver by covering it with boiling water in a dish, and letting it stand for ten minutes. Then put it, the banana, and the milk into a blender and whiz it up to form a thick, nutritious smoothie.

2 You can freeze what you don't use – pour it into an ice cube tray so you can defrost a little portion at a time.

special meals

If your cat's a bit below par (or perhaps a little above par in the weight department!), cooking one of these specially formulated meals can work wonders. Each recipe has been designed to help your cat through a particular problem – so there's a nutritious meal for the sickly cat, a low-calorie meal for the fat cat, and even a special diet for diabetic cats and those with kidney problems.

So if your cat is in need of something to get her back to full strength, have a look through this section and cook her something special!

🐾 chicken soup
– for the sickly cat

This is a great recipe for any ill cat. It's full of goodness from the chicken and veg, and it's easily eaten and digested. Make up a batch and freeze what you don't use – and then just defrost a portion whenever you think he's in need of a nutritious pick-me-up.

YOU'LL NEED

- 2 chicken drumsticks
- 1 carrot
- 1 potato
- 1 teaspoon catnip or parsley
- 1 stock cube

It's really easy this one – just cover the chicken and chopped up veg with boiling water and simmer on a low heat for thirty minutes. Then fish out the chicken, remove the bones and return the meat to the pan. Sprinkle in the catnip or parsley and allow to cool. Best served slightly warm.

☙ the white mix
– for upset stomachs

Diarrhoea and vomiting are unpleasant symptoms – both for the cat, and the owner. Treating intestinal upsets is a job for your vet, but as part of the cure, your vet will often recommend a bland diet for a few days. This recipe is ideal, as it only contains very easily digestible ingredients, and nothing likely to irritate the gastrointestinal tract. It also contains live yoghurt, which provides probiotics to help restore the correct, healthy mix of bacteria in your cat's intestine.

YOU'LL NEED (for several small meals)

- 50g rice
- 1 large dessertspoon of cottage cheese
- 1 large dessertspoon of live plain yoghurt
- 1 egg

Cook the rice according to the instructions on the packet and set aside once drained. Meanwhile, hardboil the egg (8 minutes) and remove the shell. Mash the egg into the cooled rice and add in the cottage cheese and yoghurt. Mix all together and serve in small quantities. Over the next couple of days, gradually mix in your cat's normal food as she recovers, increasing the quantity until she is back onto her normal food completely.

special meals

🐾 chicken mash
– for kidney failure

Kidney failure is an all-too-common problem for older cats and causes symptoms including excessive thirst and urination, weight loss, bad breath and vomiting. If left untreated, the disease will often progress rapidly, so it is vital to get any older cat with suspicious symptoms checked out as soon as possible.

Your vet will diagnose kidney failure using blood tests, and treat it using a combination of injections to help the body cope with the failing kidneys, tablets to increase blood flow to the kidneys and probably a special diet which has a slightly lower level of protein than normal and much less phosphorus.

Cooking for a cat with kidney failure takes a little more consideration than for a healthy cat, as it is important not to put any excess strain on the kidneys by feeding inappropriate proteins and minerals. This recipe is ideal as it's low in phosphorus, and the protein is highly digestible, meaning less waste for the kidneys to deal with.

- 250g lean chicken mince
- 250g potato
- 2 tablespoons olive oil
- ½ teaspoon ground cooked egg shells or calcium powder

Boil the potatoes until soft and then drain, add in the oil, and mash well. Meanwhile, fry the mince until cooked through. Add it, and the egg shell powder, to the mash and mix in thoroughly. Serve when cool.

NUTRITION TIP

Feeding too much raw fish can cause a deficiency in vitamin B so always cook fish for your cat.

special meals

sweet potato & tuna – for the diabetic cat

Diabetes is a disease which interferes with the body's ability to regulate the amount of sugar in the bloodstream, and feeding a suitable diet is one of the most important ways in which the disease can be controlled.

The ideal diabetes diet for a cat is high in fibre and protein, and this mix is best provided in a commercial diet specially formulated for diabetic cats. However, not all cats will eat these diets, so sometimes a little home cooked taste is required to make sure they are getting sufficient nutrients.

This recipe makes a puree of sweet potato and beef, and is ideally used mixed in with your cat's prescription diabetes diet from your vet. The sweet potato is a good source of fibre and is also known to be 'anti-diabetic' – it can reduce the amount of insulin required to treat the disease.

Make up a batch and store it in the fridge, adding a spoonful to her meals – it provides taste to get her eating her prescription food as well as a healthy balance of nutrients ideal for the diabetic cat. The recipe provides one week's worth of food for one cat.

Simply dice the sweet potato (just wash it, don't bother to peel as the peel adds more fibre) and boil it for about 7–8 minutes, until soft. Then mash, adding in the tuna, complete with oil, and the All-bran cereal. Mix thoroughly and store in the fridge, adding a small amount to each of your cat's meals.

Did you know ...
that you can buy special poultry flavoured toothpaste for your cat?

special meals

🐾 mackerel morsels – for fat cats

The chances are your cat is overweight, as nearly 60% of pet cats are above their ideal weight. Fat cats are prone to a lot of health problems including diabetes, kidney failure and arthritis, and they also suffer from a reduced quality of life – you might think your cat is having a great time lying by the fire warming his immense tum, but if the weight was off him, he'd be out climbing trees and having a much better time.

Getting the weight off your fat cat is not easy, and takes a lot of effort and willpower – from both you and the cat! You need to talk to your vet and adjust the cat's diet so that he is taking in less calories – special low calorie diets are the best way to achieve this – and also cut out any high-fat titbits and treats he might be getting.

However, it doesn't have to be all dull food and no treats for your cat on his diet – this recipe will give you some delicious treats that are low in fat and are ideal for rewarding Puss every now and then as he slims down.

YOU'LL NEED

- 1 small can mackerel in brine
- 1 cup wholegrain breadcrumbs
- 1 egg, beaten
- ½ teaspoon brewer's yeast (optional)

1 Mash up the fish in a bowl and add in the other ingredients. Mix well together and then, using wet hands, press into small balls and place onto a well-greased baking tray.

2 Cook in a moderate oven for 10 minutes. Store in an airtight container, and feed as sparingly as you can!

NUTRITION TIP

Cat food goes stale and loses its flavour very quickly, so always buy dried foods in small bags and make sure it comes in a re-sealable pouch to keep the flavour fresh.

special meals

🐾 catnip tea –
for cats with urinary problems

Lots of cats, especially indoor male cats, suffer from problems with their urinary system. This condition, know as Feline Lower Urinary Tract Disease or FLUTD, can cause very serious problems by blocking up the bladder with crystals and sludge, making it hard and painful for the cat to wee.

One of the most important features of any treatment regime is to encourage the cat to drink lots of fluids, as this helps to flush out the sludge from the system. This recipe is an ideal way of getting even the most reluctant cat to increase his water intake, as the strong taste of the infused catnip goes down a treat with most cats – so a cup of catnip tea a day will definitely keep the vet away!

Make up a pint and keep it in the fridge, giving the cat a saucer-full everyday.

Simply boil up the water, pour over the catnip, and allow to cool. Strain out the leaves with a tea strainer or sieve, and serve – biscuits are optional for the cat!

NUTRITION TIP

If your cat's a fish-lover, why not add a little fish oil to your cat's dried biscuits for an extra dose of flavour?

special meals

The Joe & Jill's Story

Home cooking for your cat is a great way of giving her high-quality food packed full of natural nutrients – but it's not the only way. With the experience I've gained from creating these recipes, and the help of Pets' Kitchen, a new natural pet food company, I've developed my own range of healthy complete foods for cats.

I've called my foods Joe & Jill's after my cat Jill who's been chief taste-tester for Pets' Kitchen. All of the diets are made using the same real, natural ingredients as I use in my home cooking, including fresh chicken and fresh salmon, and have absolutely no artificial additives at all. In fact, they're so healthy and tasty, I'm quite partial to the odd kibble with my morning tea!

My aim with Joe & Jill's has been to offer cat owners the chance to feed their pets foods which are as good as the food they eat themselves. Diet is just as crucial for our cats as it is for us, and by using the same ingredients and principles as found in the human foods, I've created a range of foods which offer our feline friends the very best in fresh, healthy nutrition.

The recipes combine my own veterinary knowledge with that of the pet nutritionists at Pets' Kitchen – and the input of Jill and many of my feline patients from the surgery!

For more information, visit the Joe & Jack's website at www.joeandjacks.co.uk.

The author

Since starring in the BBC1 hit series 'Vets in Practice', Joe Inglis has managed to juggle the demands of being a vet with a blossoming and diverse media career. This has included presenting roles in many television programmes, most notably Blue Peter, as well as writing books, and contributing to magazines and newspapers.

Joe qualified as a veterinary surgeon from Bristol University in 1996 and he is recognised as a leading authority in pet nutrition. He attributes his passion for the natural world and great spirit of adventure to being a direct descendent of Charles Darwin (his great-great-great-grandson to be precise!).

Other Joe Inglis books & DVDs

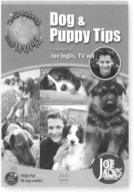

all available from **www.thegreatestintheworld.com**